3/74

P.C. SMc

1

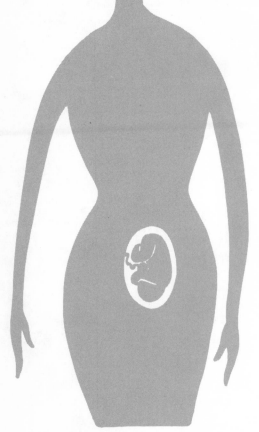

THE HUMAN BODY:

FRANKLIN WATTS, INC.
575 Lexington Avenue
New York, New York 10022

The Female Reproductive System

*Written and illustrated
by Kathleen Elgin*

For Kathy

SBN 531-01175-5

Library of Congress Catalog Card Number: 69-15879
© Copyright 1969 by Franklin Watts, Inc.
Printed in the United States of America
2   3   4   5

THE HUMAN BODY:

The Female Reproductive System

8

A living thing can produce another living
thing just like itself.
All living things can reproduce themselves.

10

Many plants drop seeds.
Seeds can sprout and grow into new plants.

Birds lay eggs.

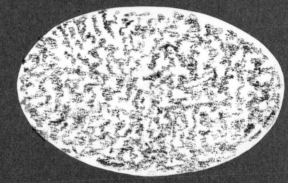

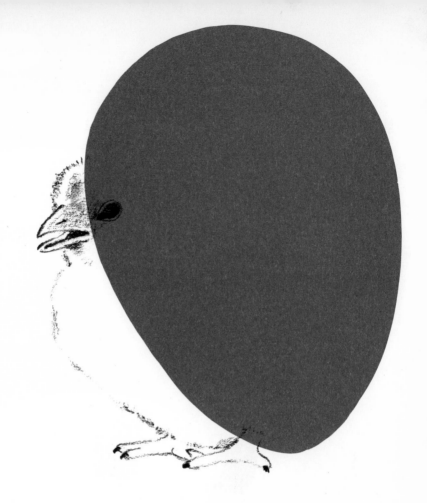

Before it is hatched, a hen's chick is shielded
   for three weeks inside a strong shell, with
   its own food supply. There it grows until
   it is ready to make its way in the outside
   world.

But seeds may fall where they never have a
   chance to sprout.

14

And an eggshell can be broken and so the
chick may never have a chance to grow.

The safest way for a young thing to start growing is within its mother's body, where it is fed and kept warm until it is big and strong enough to come forth into the world. This is how human babies develop.

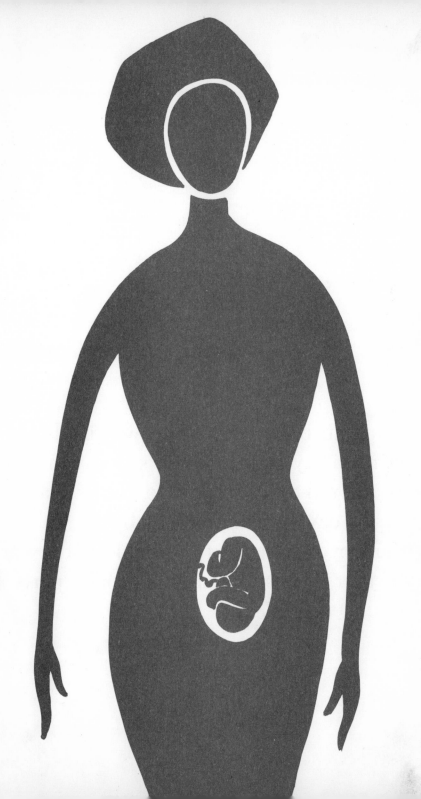

17

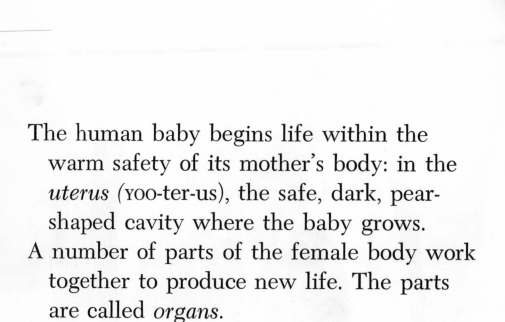

The human baby begins life within the
   warm safety of its mother's body: in the
   uterus (YOO-ter-us), the safe, dark, pear-
   shaped cavity where the baby grows.
A number of parts of the female body work
   together to produce new life. The parts
   are called *organs*.

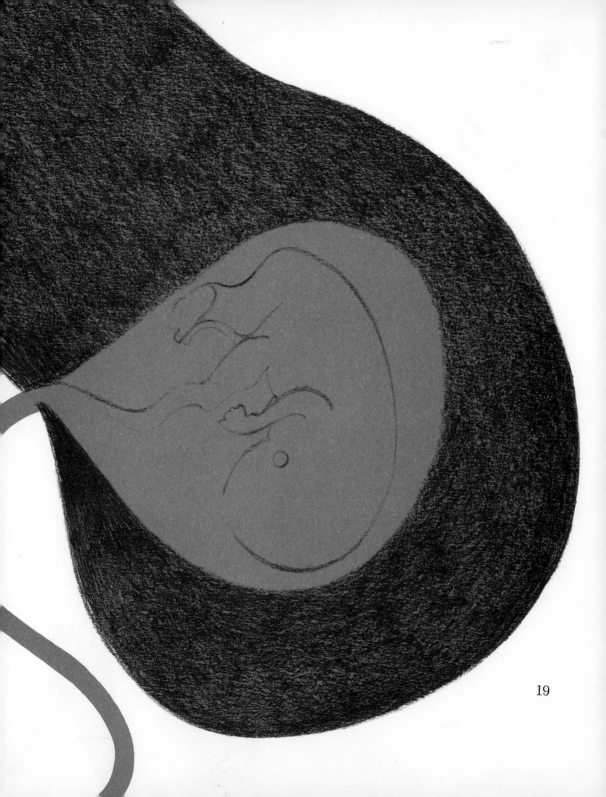

19

All these organs together make up the
female reproductive system. The uterus is
the largest organ of this system.
All organs of the female reproductive system
lie in the *pelvic cavity.*
This pelvic cavity is formed by the bowl-
shaped *pelvis.* It has strong muscular walls
and is protected by the hipbones and the
lower end of the spine.

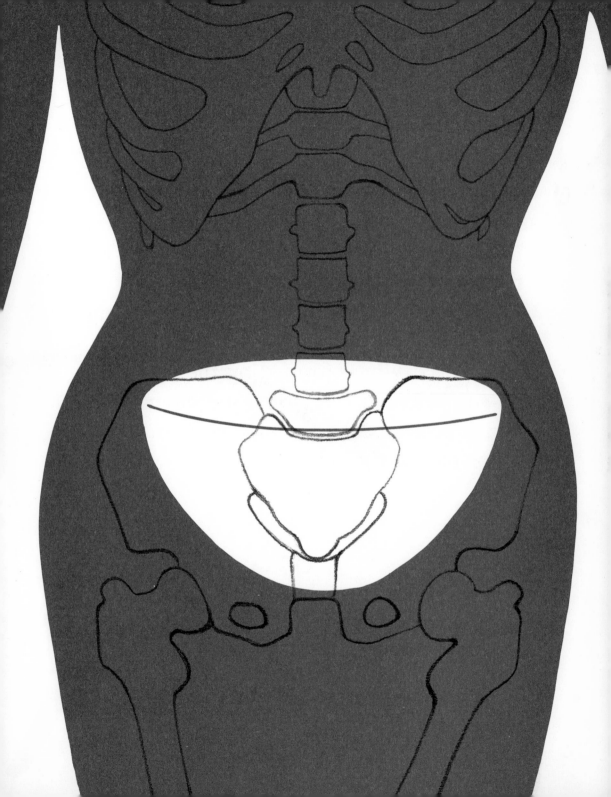

The design or arrangement of the reproductive organs looks like a bat with
outstretched wings.
The uterus looks like the body.

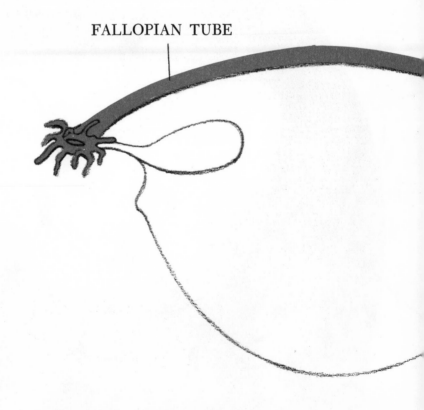

FALLOPIAN TUBE

The *Fallopian* (fal-LO-pee-an) *tubes* look like the arms.

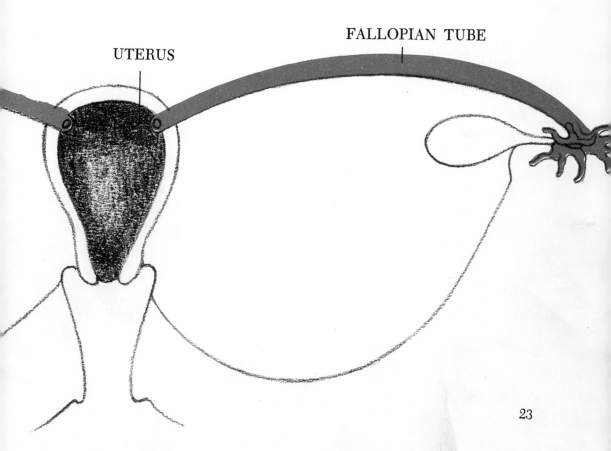

UTERUS

FALLOPIAN TUBE

23

Two parts made of thin, immensely strong
tissue, and called the *broad ligaments*, look
like the wings of the bat.
The broad ligaments are joined to the side
walls of the pelvis and so are supported
by them.

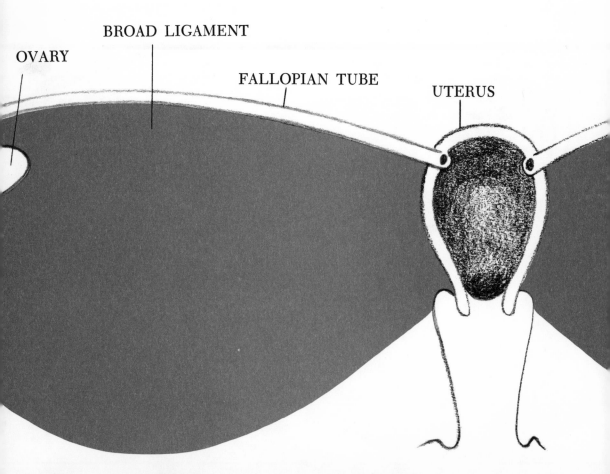

BROAD LIGAMENT

OVARY

FALLOPIAN TUBE

UTERUS

Smaller ligaments encase the *ovaries* (o-va-reez) and the important blood and nerve supply of the uterus and the ovaries.

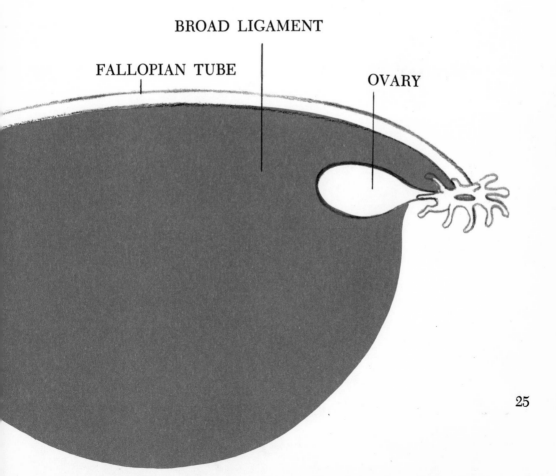

BROAD LIGAMENT

FALLOPIAN TUBE

OVARY

The ovaries are attached to the under-
surface of the Fallopian tubes.
They are two egg-shaped organs, about the
size of unshelled almonds.

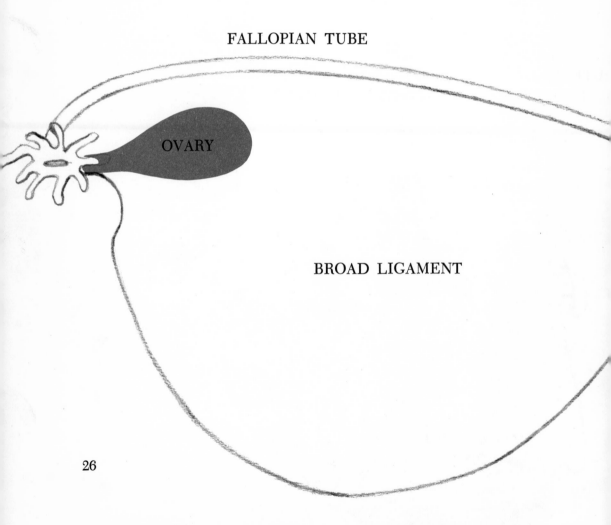

FALLOPIAN TUBE

OVARY

BROAD LIGAMENT

The ovaries hold the beginnings of life – the *ova*, or eggs.

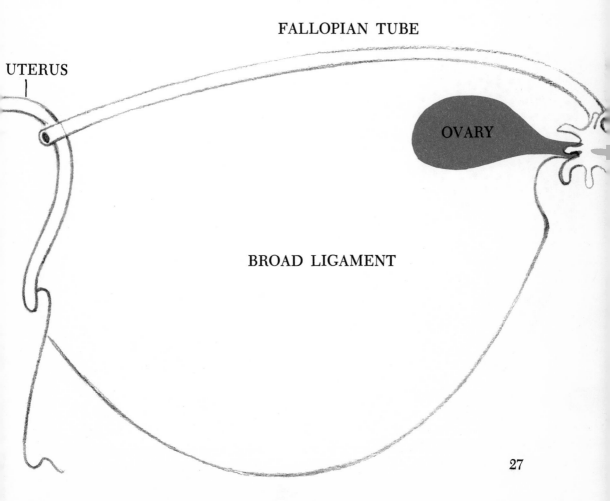

FALLOPIAN TUBE

UTERUS

OVARY

BROAD LIGAMENT

27

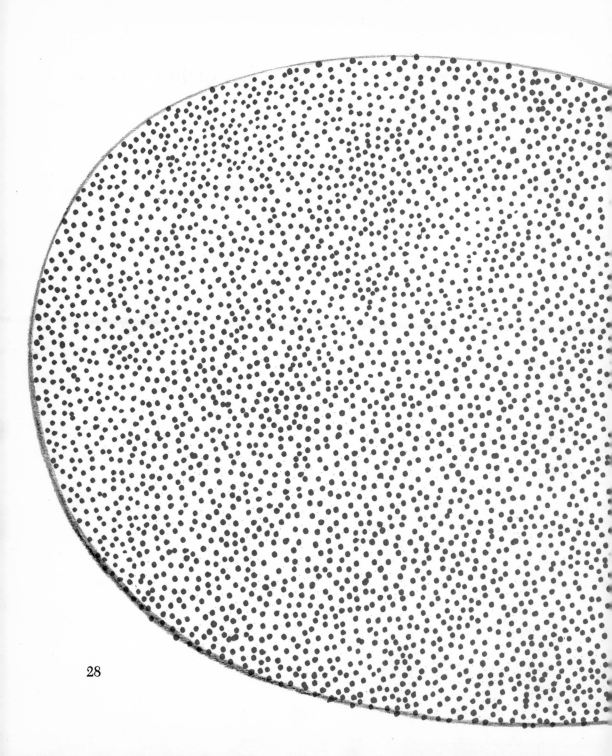

28

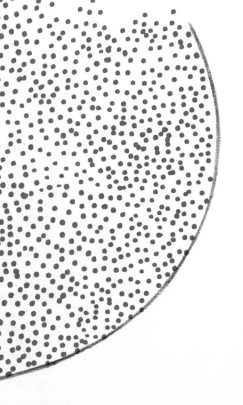

At birth, each ovary of a female child has
    several hundred thousand of these ova, or
    eggs. They are the reproductive cells.
    From them, new life can develop.
But only about four hundred of these eggs
    ripen during the years when a female can
    bear a child. The eggs ripen monthly in
    those reproductive years.

In addition to the eggs, the ovaries produce
sex hormones (HOR-mohnz). (Other glands
produce other kinds of hormones.)
Hormones are body chemicals that help
bring about growth and change.
The action of the sex hormones transforms a
girl into an adult female, with the second-
ary sex characteristics of breast and hip
development.

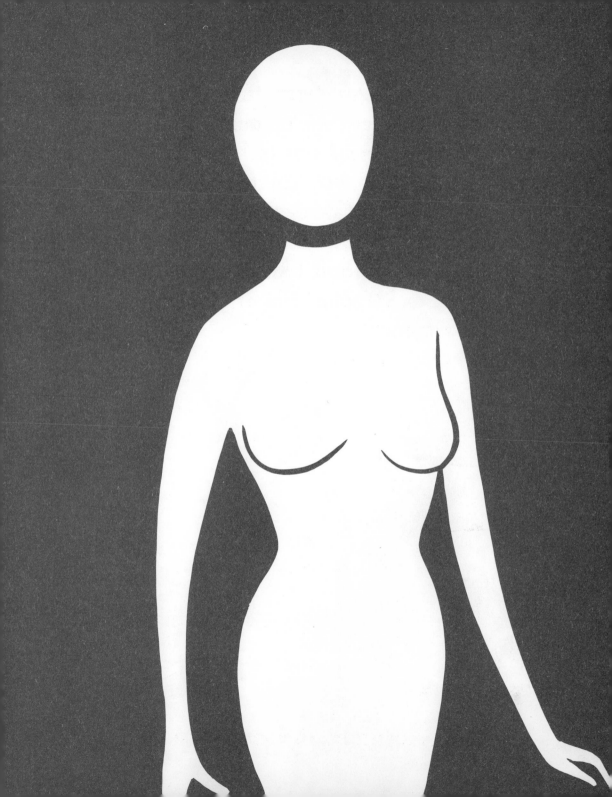

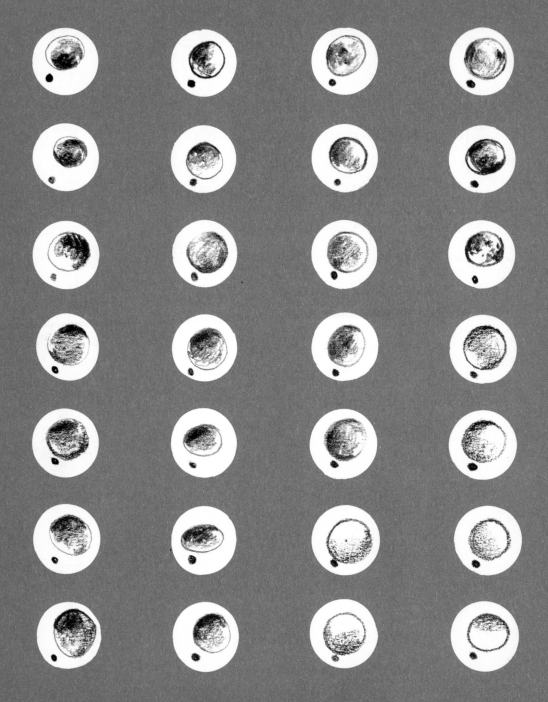

OVARY, WITH EGGS (*MUCH ENLARGED*)

At *puberty* (PYOO-ber-tee), or about the age of thirteen, the eggs, or reproductive cells of the ovaries, ripen and become mature.

In the female these eggs develop in the ovary in a regular monthly cycle. (In the male the reproductive cells, called the *sperm*, develop in the *testicles* (TESS-ti-kulz) continuously.)

The female period of egg development is known as the *menstrual* (MEN-stroo-al) *cycle*. It is usually from twenty-five to thirty days long.

Beginning at puberty, several eggs begin to
mature each month.
Only one of these eggs becomes fully
mature. It ripens during the first half of
the menstrual cycle.

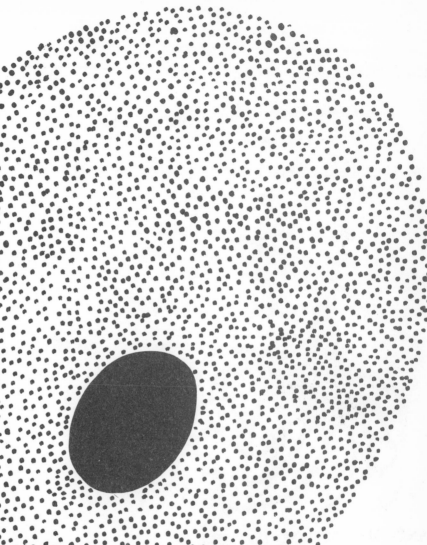

35

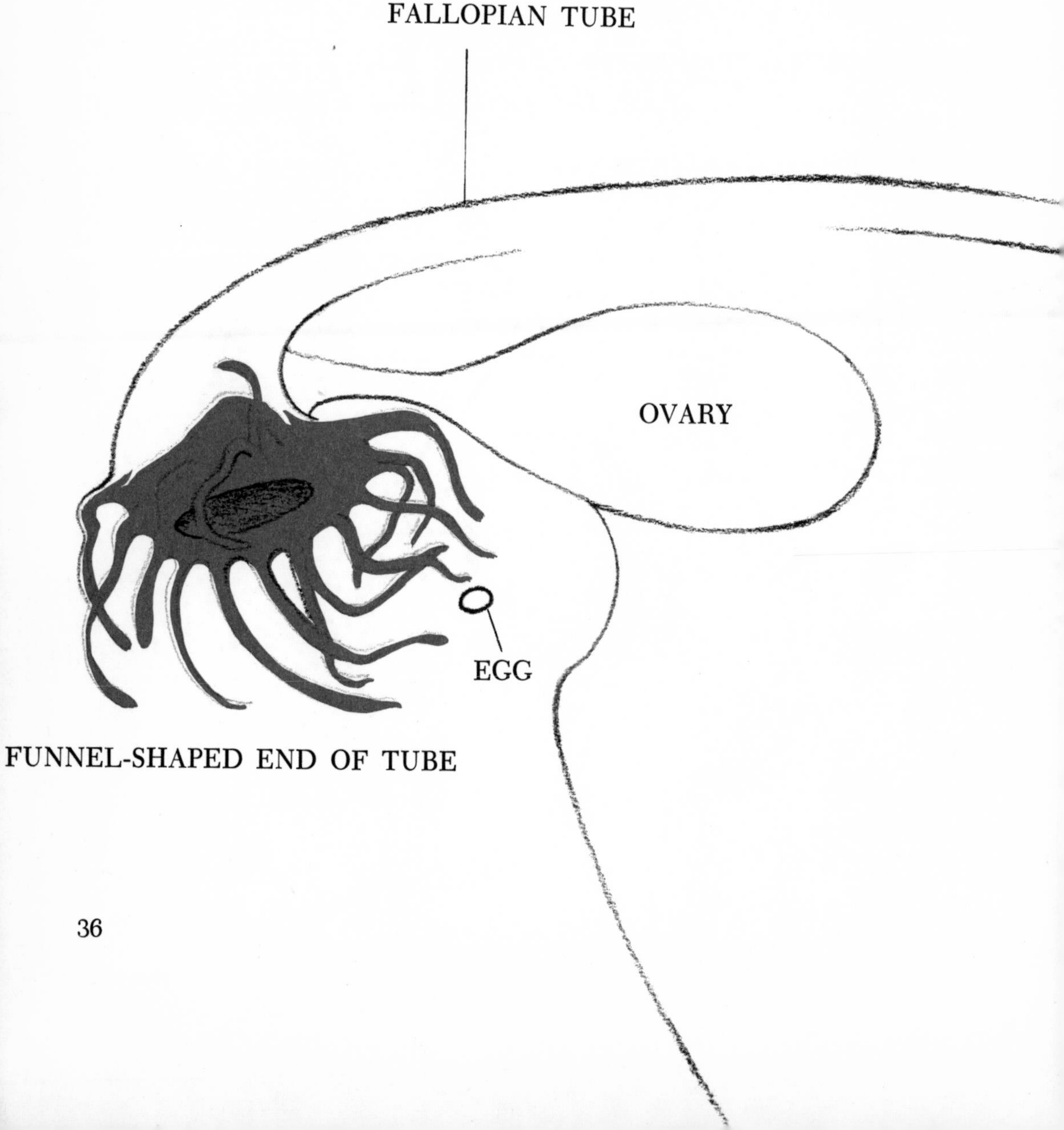

FALLOPIAN TUBE

OVARY

EGG

FUNNEL-SHAPED END OF TUBE

The Fallopian tubes have a thin muscle coat. The extreme end of each tube is funnel-shaped. A delicate fringe on the funnel reaches out to receive the egg as it falls from the ovary.

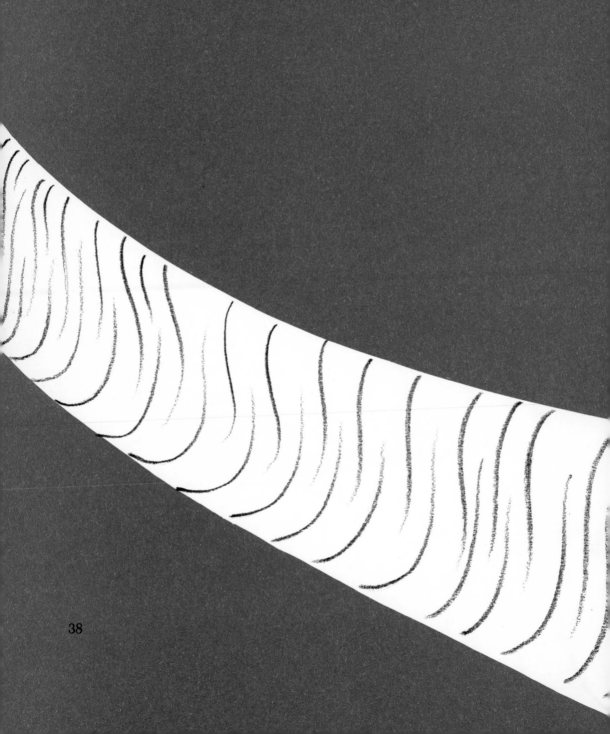

38

The lining of the Fallopian tubes has many tiny folds and hundreds of tiny hairs. Their waving motion carries the egg on its way to the uterus.

EGG

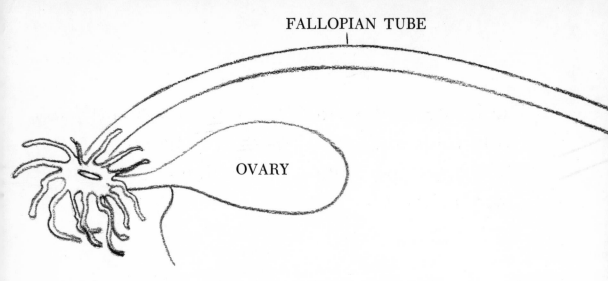

FALLOPIAN TUBE

OVARY

The inner cavity of the uterus connects with
   the Fallopian tubes above and the *vagina*
   (vaj-EYE-na) below.

The upper two-thirds of the uterus is lined
   with a layer of tissue called the *endometrium* (en-do-MEE-tree-um). This special
   tissue is found only in the part of the
   uterus where a baby can develop.

The lower third of the uterus, which
   projects into the vagina, is called the
   cervix (SER-viks).

40

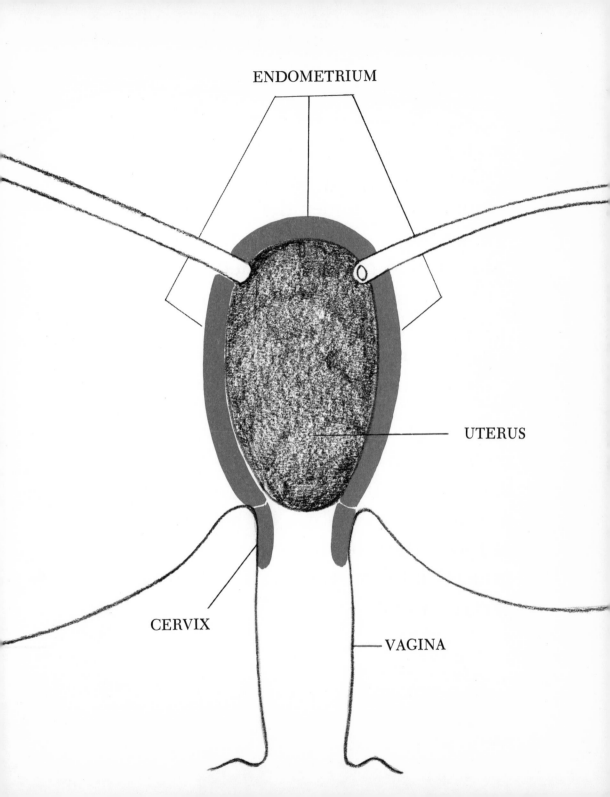

ENDOMETRIUM

UTERUS

CERVIX

VAGINA

During the first half of the menstrual cycle, while the egg is maturing, the endometrium grows under the influence of a hormone called *estrogen* (ESS-tro-jen). In the second half of the menstrual cycle, as the egg moves down the Fallopian tube toward the uterus, the ovary produces another hormone called *progesterone* (pro-JESS-ter-ohn).

ESTROGEN

PROGESTERONE

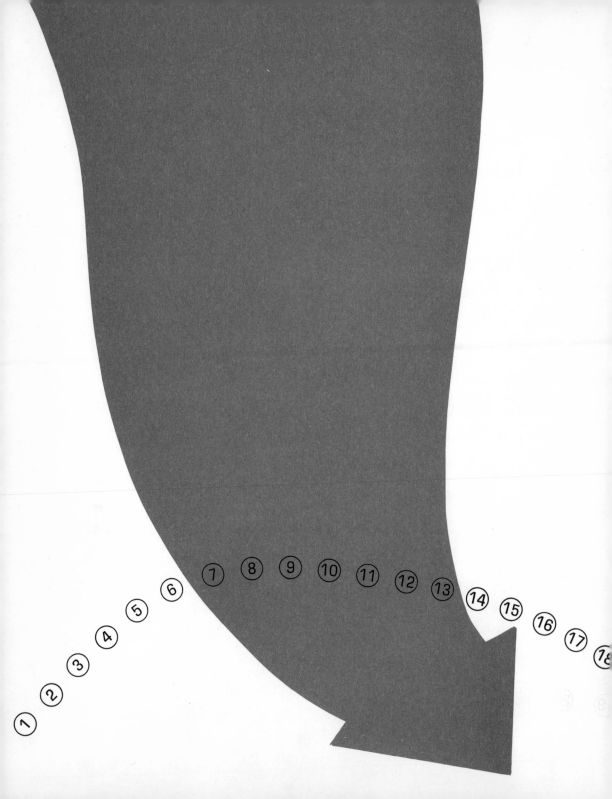

This hormone changes the endometrium.
Many blood vessels develop in it; its tissue
becomes moist, to receive the egg.
If the egg is not fertilized by male sperm
entering the body of the female, it dies.
As a result, the endometrium casts off the
soft blood tissue. The tissue goes out
through the cervix into the vagina, and
leaves the body. This process continues for
several days.
This is known as the *menstrual period*. It
occurs about every twenty-five to thirty
days.
In a short time, the lining of the uterus is
again prepared to receive another egg, and
to feed it if the egg should be fertilized
by the male sperm.

It is in the travel through the Fallopian tube
that the fertilization of the egg by the
sperm from the male reproductive system
takes place.
The union of the male sperm with the
female egg forms a fertilized cell.
In this instant a new being is conceived.

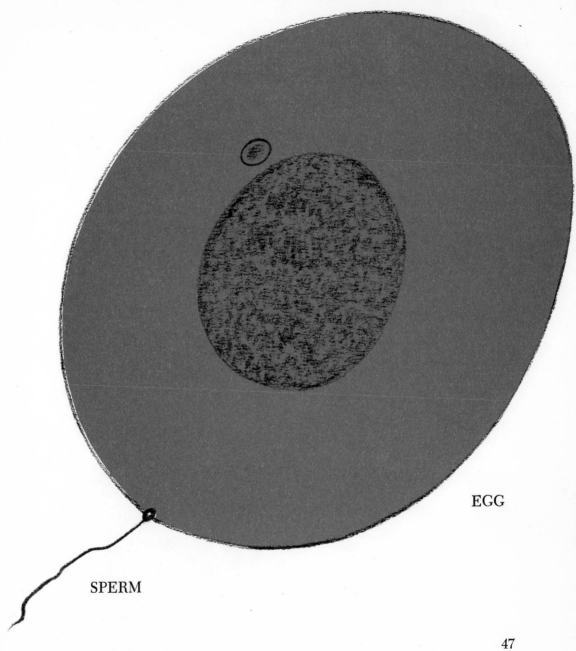

EGG

SPERM

47

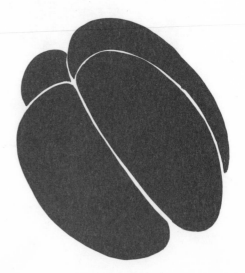

48

In the first twenty-four hours after the egg
is fertilized it divides into two cells. The
two cells divide and form four. Then the
cells begin to divide rapidly into new
cells as they are swept toward the uterus
on a journey lasting from three to six days.

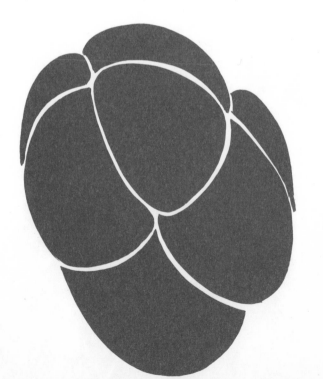

For a few days, these new cells appear exactly like the old ones, and they form a round blob called the *embryo* (EM-bree-oh). The embryo is wrapped in a fluid-filled sac and attaches itself to the endometrium, where it is fed by food from the mother's body and where it develops. Nourishment comes to the embryo through the *umbilical cord*.

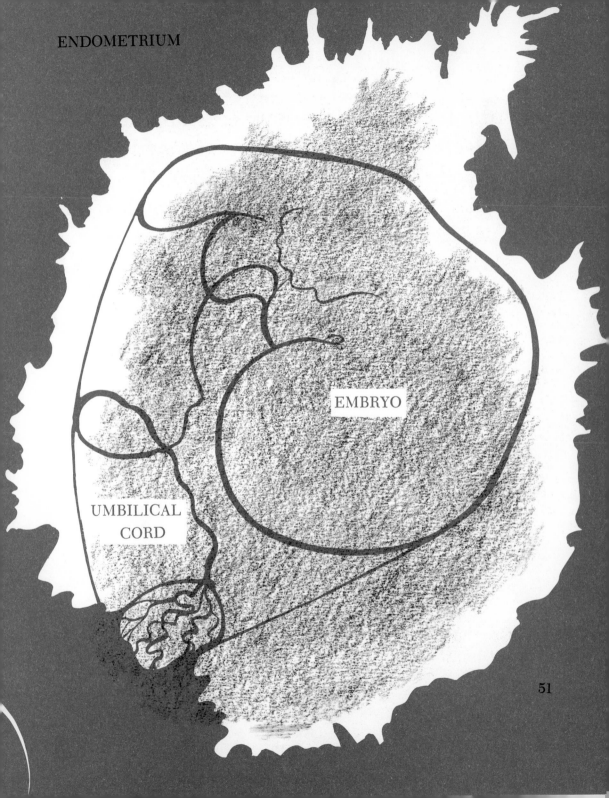

ENDOMETRIUM

EMBRYO

UMBILICAL
CORD

51

The function of the uterus is to care for the fertilized egg as it grows from an embryo into a *fetus* (FEE-tus), a small being.

At three months of age the fetus is only
about three inches long, but it is an almost
perfect miniature of a baby.

The baby grows in its safe protective cavity for the next six months – nine months in all – before it is expelled from the uterus through the vagina and into the world.

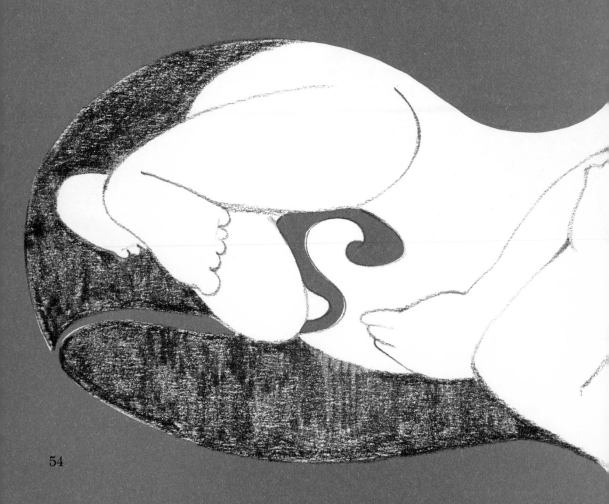

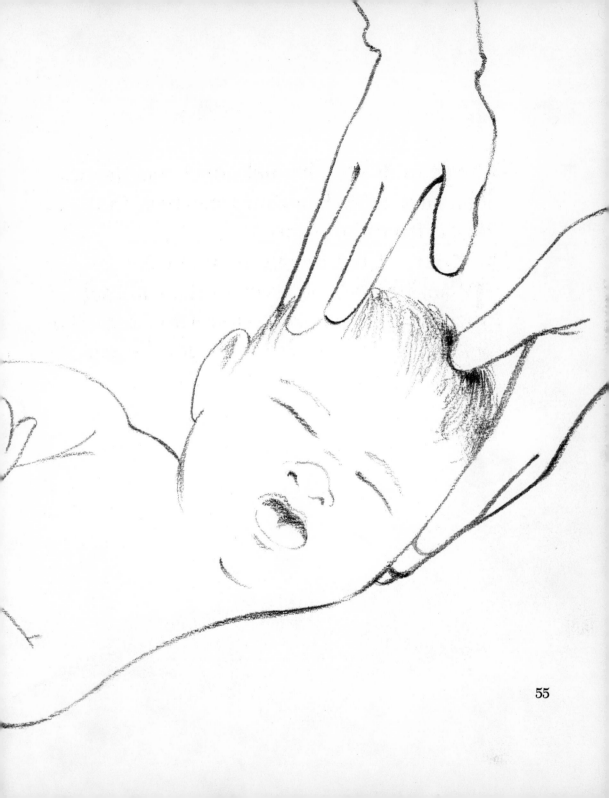

55

The vagina is the channel about four inches long that extends upward between the thighs from the exterior.

This organ of the female reproductive system, the vagina, receives the external organ of the male reproductive system, the *penis* (PEE-nis), which discharges the male sperm.

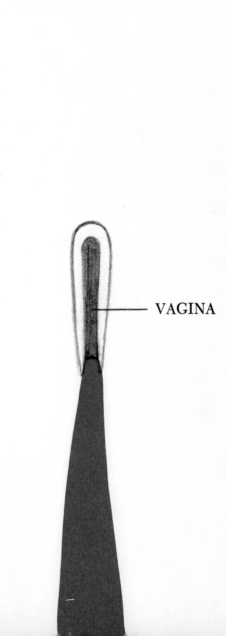

VAGINA

Another organ of the female reproductive
  system is called the *vulva* (VUL-va).
The vulva is the combination of parts that
  make up the visible organs.
The entrance to the vagina is protected and
  covered by two folds of fatty tissue called
  the *labia majora* (LAY-bee-a ma-JOR-a), which
  means "large lips." These labia are covered
  with hair, and there is more hair above
  and in front of the vulva and the labia
  majora.

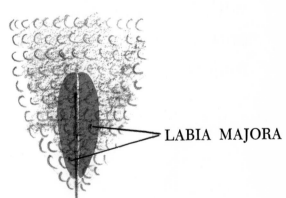

VULVA

LABIA MAJORA

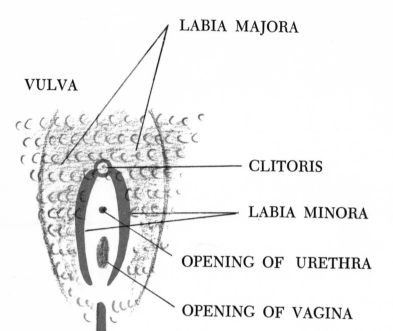

LABIA MAJORA

VULVA

CLITORIS

LABIA MINORA

OPENING OF URETHRA

OPENING OF VAGINA

The *labia minora* (LAY-bee-a mi-NOR-a), or "small lips," are two smaller protective folds which connect in front with a small replica of the male penis, called the *clitoris* (KLIT-o-ris).

The *urethra* (yoo-REE-thra), the ending canal of the *urinary* (YOO-ri-NAY-ree) *system*, opens between the clitoris and the vagina, but it has nothing to do with the reproductive system.

The particular work of the female reproductive system is the producing of ova, the harboring of fertilized eggs, and the nourishment of the growing fetus in safety until it is a fully formed baby ready for life in the outside world – the miracle of birth.

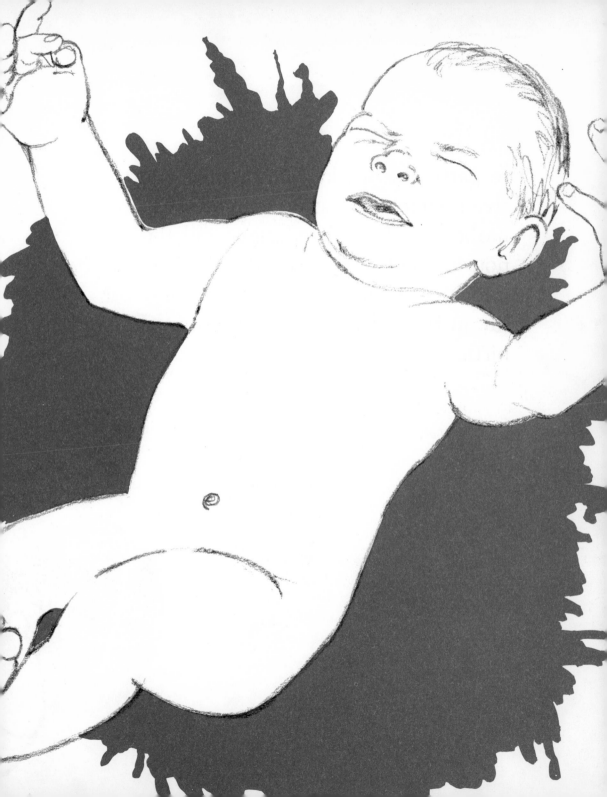

Index